Canadian First Time Home Buyers Resource Guide

Daryl B Marsden

CONTENTS

About the Author

Daryl Marsden has been in the mortgage business in Calgary, Alberta, Canada for 15 years. He started as an associate agent for the 1st year and was promoted quickly to a manager of the mortgage department for a local Calgary company.

He became a broker after 2 years in the business and partnered with another agent for the next 9 years. This partnership dissolved and Daryl opened Verico Maximum Mortgages Inc. in 2010 and continues to run his own brokerage today.

In 2003 Daryl wrote the 1st edition of **How to Save Thousands on your mortgage** which has been distributed across Canada and is still available at www.savethousandsonmortgage.com.

In 2014 Daryl wrote two follow-up books:

Fix my credit Now! available at www.fixmycreditinfo.com

Canadian First Time Home Buyers Resource Guide available at www.Canadianfirsttimehomebuyer.ca

Daryl also promotes his primary mortgage business at www.maxmort.ca or www.maximummortgages.com

Along with his books Daryl promotes the **Mortgage Benefits Program** which helps consumers to save money on the closing costs on a mortgage and home purchase transaction. Using a portion of the commissions to help reimburse clients some of the costs of buying a new home. To find out more on this please visit his site at www.Mortgagebenefitprogram.ca

With his team of associates and his marketing team Daryl continues to be a great asset to any Canadian looking for a mortgage. His expertise has allowed him to deal with just about every type of consumer and mortgage deal possible.

Since using a mortgage broker is FREE, in most cases, you should not hesitate to call or e-mail Daryl anytime with regards to your current or next mortgage.

You can reach Daryl at: daryl@maxmort.ca

Or visit the website at www.maxmort.ca

Other books by Daryl Marsden

How to save Thousands on your mortgage

Available at www.Savethousandsonmortgage.com

Fix my credit Now!

Available at www.fixmycreditinfo..com

Verico Maximum Mortgage Inc.

VMMI is a Calgary, Alberta, Canada mortgage brokerage licensed with the Real Estate Council of Alberta since 2010.

With 3 active full time mortgage brokers producing over $100,000,000 annually in the mortgage business throughout Canada.

Daryl Marsden is the broker of record for VMMI with the head office located at:

#308, 5149 Country Hills Boulevard N.W.

Calgary, Alberta, Canada

T3A 5K8

Website: www.maxmort.ca

e-mail: Daryl@maxmort.ca

We welcome all Canadians or anyone interested in obtaining a mortgage in Canada to give us a call or visit our sites and ask any questions you may have. We would be pleased to discuss your individual situation anytime.

Introduction

First Time Home buyers or (FTHBs) are an important part of every economy in the world. In North America they drive the economy during good times and bad.

Building new homes or condos for them is a major part of the economy. Just think of all the things that go into a home. With each item you think of, there are hundreds of jobs created to build or service that item after you buy it.

The house or condo is the first major investment most people make in their life except maybe their car. Incredibly enough some cars have similar value to homes. The difference is that vehicles tend to be a depreciating asset while houses or condos tend to appreciate.

Everyone dreams of owning their own home.

If you work, have decent credit, can save up a down payment or even borrow it from a relative you can own your own home.

Many people believe they are destined to rent for the rest of their lives. This is not the case; you can buy a home using your savings, borrowed funds from family or even your retirement savings, at least in Canada.

In Canada you can use your RRSP (registered Retirement Savings Plan) under the Homebuyer Plan as part of your down payment. You borrow your own money to help buy your first home. The government then gives you 15 years to repay yourself for this loan. For more detailed information on this program follow this link: http://www.cra-arc.gc.ca/E/pub/tg/rc4135/README.html

Both the Canadian and the United States governments want you to buy a home as it means both economies continue to move along keeping thousands of people working.

Yes, even with all the new rules implemented in both countries they really do want you to get your own home. The rules they implemented were designed to help the struggling economies get back on to a more solid footing.

The future looks bright as both Canada and the United States are well on their way to recovery (at least in the fall of 2014). Canada has implemented some tough new rules for first time home buyers. The US has also written some tougher rules. These were all done in the hopes of never having a crisis as we did in 2009 through 2013.

Now is a great time to buy your first home

Things are looking better with each passing month and this book is written to help guide you through the process to buying your first home.

The first step to your home buying future is to ensure your credit is in good shape. Let's start the journey to your new home.

The 5 C's of Credit

When it's time to borrow we all go through a nervous period. Even those with perfect credit will break a sweat when applying for credit. They may put on a look of confidence but everyone has a little fear about the outcome of requesting credit.

Lenders tend to rely of 5 basic principles when evaluating you for credit. These are the basics we all must demonstrate in order to make the lender feel confident in lending you money or credit.

They want to ensure you will repay your debt in full, on time, and as promised.

The lenders will consider the 5 c's of your situation in one way or form. Each will put a higher priority on each of the C's. In no particular order here they are:

Character

Your character is based on a few items, first impressions count! If meeting in person take this into consideration, dress well and ensure cleanliness.

They will evaluate your background and your experience in your current work and living arrangements. The longer you have worked for a company or owned your own business the better your chances.

The longer you have lived at the same address the more reliable you become in their eyes.

Don't be fooled this is a large factor in their review.

Capital

What do you bring to the game? How much money have you saved to prove you are serious about asking for a loan? This is normally the down payment when buying large items like cars, and homes.

Capital is also reviewed from your overall savings and saving habits. The larger your assets in cash and investments are, the better you look to lenders.

What do you have to fall back on in case of an emergency like job loss or emergency expense? Can you pay your bills for a while if you lost your income source for a few months?

These are all questions lenders ask before granting credit.

Collateral

This is the security you have available to ensure the lender can recover in case you default or fail to pay as you have agreed on. In most cases this is related to the reason you are requesting the loan.

Real estate is a main source of security for land and home deals. The vehicle for car loans and even furniture for household furnishing loans all become the collateral for loans.

If you fail to make your promised payments the lender can take action through the courts to regain ownership and control of the collateral. They use the courts to do this and once they have control of the assets they sell it to try to recoup the loss.

These steps cost money and a lender only resorts to this as a last step. Many are willing to discuss new terms to help provide you with leeway when things get tough.

Communication is critical when things start to look bad. Always remember to talk to the lender and ask for help and advice when things get tough.

Credit

This is the third party evaluation of your past history and a light prediction of what your near future habits will be.

Your history is recorded through up to 3 National reporting agencies in North America. This is discussed in full later in the book.

You are evaluated over your last 6 to 7 years history with the last 12 months being the most critically looked at. The last 12 months determine your current credit history and can be a good predictor of your next 12 months.

The credit agencies will keep your history on file for 6 to 7 years. In some cases they will keep it longer when dealing with bankruptcies and foreclosures.

Missed or late payments are very damaging to your credit history. My advice to my clients is that you always try to make the minimum payment on all accounts. By doing this you never have a late or missed payment.

If you have a history of late or missed payments especially in the last 12 months you hurt your chances of being approved. In most cases this is enough to decline you.

You can appeal these decisions but appealing is the last resort and should be only used when you have to.

Capacity

This is one of the leading factors with lenders. Your ability to repay the loan is a critical factor. Based on your current credit and commitments are you capable of taking on this increased debt?

Lenders use your debt ratios to evaluate your ability to repay your loans or lines of credit. If all your carrying costs are less than or equal to 32% of your total monthly income then you are in a good position. If over 40% than you may suffer possible default in the future as you are heavily extended.

How you make your income is also important to lenders and they will evaluate this in detail. If you have multiple sources of income they will take this into consideration.

There is one other C that is not normally mentioned but is always considered:

Conditions

This C refers to the current economy in the area of the lender. Since lenders tend to be either national or regional, lenders will take into consideration what is happening with the local economy in your area.

If the country or region is having good job growth and showing signs of strong consumer purchasing and buying this becomes a factor in making a loan.

If the region has lost a main employer or there is a looming recession lenders will hold back funds and will restrict access to only good or great risks.

Rising interest rates and falling jobs numbers can cause lenders to carefully evaluate all loans. The good news is that the government still provide incentives and programs to help consumers during these tough times.

Buying consumers are critical to all country's economies. When you stop buying things the economy starts slowing down. We need everyone to keep buying regular necessities plus the odd luxury item as this is what drives business.

There you have it the 5 or should I say the 6 C's of Credit.

Determining how you rank in these C's is an important first step to consider when applying or rebuilding your credit.

No matter where you are at now, by carefully managing these 6 factors you can maintain or rebuild any credit situation. It does take time to rebuild but starting over is a part of all our lives and worth the effort for a more comfortable future.

We all have the ability to start over. You can't fail unless you give up and quit trying.

You will find a general review of credit maintenance and rebuilding and can get more detailed information and resources at our website:

Your Credit Score

Your credit score follows you silently throughout your whole life. It is used by all lenders and credit grantors and is recorded and monitored by private agencies worldwide.

We are all rated using a variety of methods and this is then shared with legitimate lenders and credit granting companies.

We all have a social insurance number, birth date and name. This is how you are tracked by the three leading credit reporting agencies.

- **Equifax**
- **Transunion**
- **Experian** (mainly used in the United States)

Each of these organizations will normally have a record of you if you are based in the USA. If in Canada, Equifax and Transunion are the normal reporting agencies.

Equifax and TransUnion are the two main reporting agencies in both countries. However, you want to request your annual report from all if you live in the USA or Equifax and Transunion if in Canada.

The next chapter will go into more detail about these firms and how to access and review your personal information.

What is good credit and what is bad credit?

You may have guessed that if you pay your bills on time as promised you will have good credit. If you fail to pay your bills on time and have late payments or missed payments you will have bad credit.

You are right, these are the two factors used in determining your credit score especially in the last 12 months of your credit history but not the only factors taken into consideration.

You may never miss a payment or have never been late, but if you are at or over your credit limit and you have thousands of dollars of outstanding credit you can be rated as a bad credit risk.

Paying your bill on time as promised is important but there are more steps to consider when maintaining and rebuilding your credit. You need to work on managing your credit and your credit limits. By doing so you will maintain your good credit score and can also increase the speed your credit will be rebuilt.

If you fail to make your payments or have a habit of being late you will have a bad credit score. If you constantly go over your credit limit or hover around it. You will have a lower credit score and a tough time getting or keeping credit.

Bad credit implications

With poor credit management and maintenance you will suffer now and in the future. Bad credit can result in not being able to get certain job opportunities. You can suffer embarrassment from friends, family and it can and will restrict your future opportunities in life.

Your dream of a new car or new home can disappear in only a few short months if you fail to manage your credit.

The good news is that it can always be rebuilt but this takes time and that normally means anywhere from 12 to 24 months. In some cases longer depending on how bad you allow your situation to get.

Where do credit agencies get my information?

The first place is from your application when you apply for credit. This is the initial starting point for all 3 agencies. This information is shared by the lender, credit card companies and with the credit bureaus/agencies when you apply for credit.

Their information is kept current through your applications and through public records. The local courts and provincial or states government agencies make your public information available to anyone that wants to search for it and has reason to need it.

If you have had a collection or judgement registered against you, this is public knowledge and is made available to anyone that wants to search for it.

The major lenders and credit grantors along with collection agencies will send their credit files electronically to the reporting agencies/bureaus. They do this every month to report your account numbers, outstanding balances, and credit limits.

They use a 9 point scale system for reporting your current and past status. They do this for both your installment credit accounts and your revolving credit accounts.

Installment accounts are for car loans, mortgages or personal loans. Revolving accounts are credit cards, gas cards and store credit accounts.

The scale is based on (I) for Installments or (R) for revolving accounts

R/I 0: Account is too new to report or recently approved but not used

R/I 1: Account pays on time or within 30 days of billing. Pays as agreed

R/I 2: Account is paid in more than 30 days, but less than 60 days or one payment is due at this time.

R/I 3: Account is paid in more than 60 days but less than 90 days or is two payments late.

R/I 4: Account is paid in more than 90 days but not more than 120 days or is three payments late.

R/I 5: Account is at least 120 days past due. It is not yet rated as a collection

R/I 6: This code has no meaning as it really doesn't exist

R/I 7: This means the account payments are being made under a consolidation order or debt repayment program.

R/I 8: This means repossession or voluntary return of the merchandise has taken place.

R/I 9: This stipulates a bad debt and it has been placed for collection or the account has been skipped with little to no chance of collection.

Every account is rated on the above system with each credit reporting agency. Each agency may report accounts differently as it all depends on when the last update was made.

What is a FICO or BEACON score?

The FICO or BEACON score was developed by the credit grantors to help in a quick rating score. The lowest being 300 to 400 and the highest being 850 to 900, it depends on your country and which agencies you are dealing with.

The score provides the lender or credit grantor with a snapshot of your credit rating. The higher your score the better the risk and the easier it is to get credit.

The score is figured using algorithms which take into consideration a number of factors. All these are calculated and a score is then made available for each report requested.

How long do ratings good or bad, stay on my report?

This can vary with each report agency but in general the following is a guideline. Please note this is an ever changing guideline and should not be used without confirming with each credit reporting agency. They are happy to answer your questions.

Account History

Credit request for your file information: A credit request history will automatically purge or disappear normally after 3 years from the first date of the inquiry.

Credit History and Banking History: All transactions will purge or disappear normally after 6 years from the date of the last activity or payment. This is only on the accounts that are reported. Some agencies do not report all account.

Orderly Payment of debts or credit counselling: These types of reports normally only stay on for 3 years from the last payment date.

Consumer Proposals: When you have completed the proposal and it is fully paid it will be registered and this normally reports for 3 years from the date of payment

Judgements, Garnishments and Seizures: These normally stay registered for 6 to 7 years from the date they were originally filed

Bankruptcy: These will report for 6 to 7 years from the date the bankruptcy is officially discharged. All accounts listed in the bankruptcy will also report for the same time period. If a person has had multiple bankruptcies these will report up to 14 years along with the debts that are part of the bankruptcy.

Collections Accounts: These will report for up to 6 years from the date of the last activity.

Secured Loans: These report for up to 6 years from date of last activity

Please note all these situations are capable of changing without notice. This information is what was available at the time of this writing. If you want to confirm this information please call your credit reporting agency.

Please also note that certain provinces in Canada and states in the US may allow for a longer reporting period. You must check with the credit reporting agency in your area to confirm.

It is highly advisable that you go to each credit reporting agency and review their procedures and online information as it is possible things will change in our ever changing world.

I highly recommend you at least logon to each site so you are familiar with them. The next chapter will go into detail about each site and how to do things on them.

Your Income and Employment

With any loan or mortgage, a critical factor is how you will pay it back. Your income history is important to a mortgage lender. In this chapter I will cover the two types of income the banks want to see with everyone that is applying for a mortgage.

Employment Income:

This type of income is described as working for someone that is collecting and paying your income taxes and other benefits to the government.

You receive a regular check weekly, every two weeks, twice a month, or in some cases once a month.

This employer collects the income taxes and pays them to the government for you. This is the standard definition of employment income.

Some folks are paid on a contract basis. If the contract includes the company paying your personal taxes and other benefits for you, then this is considered regular employment.

If you are required to collect and pay your own taxes and benefits the lenders consider you to be Self Employed. This is the second type of income allowed.

Self-Employment Income:

The simple definition of being self-employed is to ask yourself "Who pays my taxes to the government"?

If the company pays it then you are employed, if you pay it then you are self-employed.

If you incorporated a company and your T4 yourself and you can prove the the company pays your income taxes each month then you will be treated similar to an employed person.

In most cases you will be asked for your last two years personal income taxes to prove a 2 year average of your income.

What type of paperwork will you need to provide to prove your income?

Employed Income:

Employed people will need to provide a job letter that states your position, salary, and your length of employment.

You will also be required to provide a copy of your last one or two paystubs to confirm the information on the job letter.

All lenders will take the extra step to call and confirm the information on the job letter and on your pay stub.

If you are on a probation period of any sort, you must be out of the time period before a mortgage will be granted.

The lenders want at least a 3 year work history so be prepared to provide that history in detail.

Self Employed Income:

For self-employed people the paperwork needed is more intense. The reason for this is your income is much more difficult to prove as many people will try to write off as much as they can. This reduces your total annual income and what you owe the tax man.

The problem here is that the lenders require a two year history of your self-employed income. If you write off everything to lower your declared income this means your income for qualifying will also be very low and limit your ability to buy your new home.

Self-employed people will need to provide their last two years personal tax returns and your personal Notice of Assessments. These are the forms you get back after you file your tax returns. The Notice of Assessments proves the government agrees with your last tax return.

Most lenders will also ask for 1 to 2 years of your company business financials as well to prove the company actually exists. They want to ensure you are the owner of the owners of the company and that the company is a profitable venture.

You will also be required to prove that you do not owe any taxes to the government. If you do owe them then you should make arrangements to pay any outstanding taxes before applying for a mortgage.

The reason for this is because only the government can seize your home above the bank. If you fail to pay the government they can force you to sell your home in order to pay these taxes. Lenders hate this so they ensure you do not owe any before granting a mortgage.

Normally lenders will require two full years of tax returns from the business

Since you are new in your business the lenders want at least a two year history to prove the income you make in your business. If you have been in business this long you have no issue.

If you have less than 2 years in business it becomes very difficult to provide a two year history.

Some lenders will allow you to use employment income from the previous year if you are in the same field as you were currently self-employed in. For example if you were a plumber working for a company and then started your own company, some lenders will allow you to use your last year of income and your first year's income from your self-employment to calculate a two year average.

This still means you must have at least one year personal taxes to prove you have been in business for one year. Then they will allow you to use your last year's income from your job as long as it was in the same field and you can provide proof of this.

There you have it

There are many types of income that we earn in life but they all fit into one of these two categories. I can already hear you statement "but mine is". Unfortunately the lenders only see these two categories and will fit you into either one once they are given the proof listed above.

Now is a good time to gather your paperwork if you are self-employed and provide it to your broker or banker to review ahead of time.

The reason for this is to avoid wasting your time finding a new home only to find out you can't qualify.

I would be pleased to discuss this further if you are looking to buy in Canada. Unfortunately I am unable to do mortgages in the USA so I can't really help you with qualifications in this area.

If you are buying in Canada please don't hesitate to e-mail me at:

Daryl@maxmort.ca or visit our website at www.maxmort.ca

Debt Servicing: Can you afford your new home?

Once you have proven your income source you now must prove your ability to make your future mortgage payments.

To do this the lender will want to know all your current debts, car loans, lines of credit, and credit cards. All consumer debts will be used in calculating your debt servicing ratios.

All lenders work with your debt ratios to calculate what you can afford when buying your new home. They use two debt ratios:

1. GDS: Gross Debt Servicing
2. TDS: Total Debt Servicing

The first thing lenders look at is your monthly housing costs and this ratio should not be more than 32%. Housing costs include monthly mortgage principle and Interest payments along with the property taxes and the heating expense based on the new home you want to purchase.

If you are buying a condo they also take into consideration 50% of the condo fees.

Lenders add these all up to determine your percentage of your gross monthly income. This figure is known as:

GDS: GROSS DEBT SERVICING

The simple math for this is:
Your gross monthly income (before taxes) $
Your spouse's gross monthly income $
Any other monthly income, investments and such $
Sub Total all the incomes $
Multiply the Sub total of all incomes by 0.32 to equal your GDS Ratio =

The second rule is taking into account your entire monthly debt load and it should not be more than 40% of your gross monthly income. Having said that most lenders can stretch this to 42% if you have good credit scores over 700 on the beacon score.

This ratio is called the:

TDS: TOTAL DEBT SERVICING

The math for this is:

Add all housing costs, credit cards, car loans, lines of credit and any other debt owed.

Take the total monthly income from the GDS sub total $

Multiply this total by 0.40 to get the TDS =

These ratios are the important ones to all lenders

If your ratios are in line with what I described above and your credit score is decent there is a very good chance you will be pre-approved for your new home.

If the ratios are above these maximum amounts, lenders will scale back your pre-approval amount or may even decline the file altogether. They may also ask for a co-signer to go on the file with you to help provide more stability for the loan.

It is very important to know what your ratios are as you can lower them by doing some simple debt repayment. The best way to lower high debt ratios is either with more income or by paying down debt. Even consolidation is a good thing if it lowers the minimum payment on your debt.

Be aware of your debt ratios when looking to buy a home. If you find this hard to figure out than get a pre-approval done with a mortgage broker or bank. If you would like to get a pre-approved mortgage now or discuss further please email me at Daryl@maxmort.ca I would be pleased to answer any questions you may have and help you get pre-approved.

Please note I can only help folks in Canada as we are not allowed to do mortgages in the United States.

Down Payments and their sources

Every real estate purchase you make will require a down payment. The main purpose of the down payment is to show your intent to buy your new home. Even better if you can prove you have saved for it over time.

Lenders like to see you save for the down payment as mentioned in the 5 C's of Credit. It helps in getting approved for your new mortgage and home purchase.

Down payments come from a variety of sources:

1. Saved funds in investments, savings and chequing accounts
2. Registered Retirement Saving Plans (RRSP)
3. Gifts from relatives
4. Funds from a company account you own
5. Funds from the sale of an asset
6. Borrowed funds

These are the 6 main categories for down payment sources. Let's look at them in a bit more detail.

Saved Funds: Investments, savings, chequing accounts

This is an easy one to explain. Lenders look for a 90 day history of where your funds have been sitting.

If in a chequing or savings account, you need to provide the last 3 months bank statements. At least one of those statements must have your name and the account number listed on it. This links you to the account and down payment source.

If you have Guaranteed Certificates or Bonds you will need to prove when they were bought, and the value upon sale for your down payment. You will be asked to prove those funds are deposited into your account after being sold or redeemed.

Registered Retirement Saving Plans:

The government of Canada has a program for saving for your retirement called the RRSP program or Registered Retirement Savings Program. You are allowed to contribute a certain percentage of your income into a plan that defers the income taxes on this income until a future time when you will withdraw it, normally in your retirement years.

To help people buy a home, they allow First Time home buyers or people that have not owned a home in the last 5 years to use up to $25,000 of your RRSP as your down payment.

You can only do this after your RRSP has been on deposit for at least 90 days with a registered savings plan.

You are allowed to withdraw these funds as a loan to yourself. You must use it for the down payment of your new home. You are required to complete a form, normally done by the bank or investment firm that holds your RRSP.

They complete a Homebuyers withdrawal form. This form is sent to the government to let them know you have withdrawn the funds from your RRSP program.

You now have up to 15 years to pay this money back to yourself. Each year you must pay a certain portion back to yourself. You do this by purchasing another RRSP and declaring it each year as your repayment to your Homebuyers program.

You can delay starting payments for up to 2 years. This would mean you must pay the loan back in 13 years so the annual payment to yourself is larger.

If you fail to make your annual payment each year your personal taxes will be reassessed and that payment amount for that year will be added to your income and the taxes will become owed. You may also have a penalty for a late payment of your taxes. A great program if you have RRSP savings

Gifts from Relatives:

Many families want to help their children or even other family members to buy their first home. They do this by providing a gift of the down payment to their family member.

This is acceptable as long as this gift is documented and proven. This is done by all parties signing a gift letter that is dated for the same date that the money being gifted is deposited into the bank account.

The letter should be dated for the same period the money is given to the first time home buyer. The buyer then provides a copy of their bank statement that proves the cash is in their account. **It is important that this statement has the buyers name and account number on it so it can be linked to the First Time Home Buyer.**

In some cases the lenders will want to see proof of where the gifted funds have been on deposit. The gift giver must than provide the same 90 days proof of where they have had the funds.

Not all lenders require this but it is becoming a more common request with gifts. The reason for this is to help prevent fraud from illegal activities of criminals.

Money laundering is a real issue with lenders and banks and they have government regulations to provide full proof of all large down payments. This is especially true of large gifts from relatives.

The bad guys like to launder their money by buying homes and then selling them in the future.

Gifts are still a practise done every day. Its best to be aware of what will be needed to prove the gift if you will be receiving one.

Funds from a company account that you own:

This source is used by self-employed individuals. Many self-employed people have a great deal of equity and money invested in their business. These funds are normally in a bank account.

Since they are in a bank, the lenders want the same 90 days of bank statements with the company name and account number listed.

The only hitch is that you must now prove that you own the company. This is normally done by incorporation paperwork, business licenses or personal tax returns that show the company name. Anything that can connect you to the ownership of the company can be used as proof you own the company.

Funds from the sale of an asset:

Many people will be selling something to help get the money for their new down payment. Selling homes, cars, boats, motorbikes, even animals and businesses for their new down payment.

When you sell an asset you will normally record this sale on paper or in some form. You will need to provide the full paperwork from the sale of the assets. You then must prove the money is deposited into your bank account with a statement connecting you to that account.

A good tip here is to ensure the sale amount is the amount deposited into your account and close to the date on the sales contract. This is acceptable to the lenders. You may have to explain how lower or larger amounts are deposited into your account if they do not match up to the sales contract you provide as proof.

Borrowed Funds:

This is a tricky one, borrowed funds come with a premium if you are putting down less than 20%. There is a premium added by the mortgage insurers on any borrowed down payments. This is normally .20% added to the mortgage insurer's premium.

In the next chapter and in the 3 types of insurance chapter you will learn about mortgage insurers, how they work and their benefits. Many first time home buyers have less than 20% down payment so mortgage insurers are a critical part of the plan and we have a separate chapter on them.

You can use borrowed funds for your down payment but they must be declared and proven just like all other sources of down payments. You also must debt service the loan payment or credit card payment. This means the lender will include your estimated payment with all your other monthly payments to ensure you can debt service the new mortgage as explained in "Can you afford to buy your new home".

You will need to provide proof of where you will borrow the funds from and at what interest rate you must repay these funds. You can do this with the most recent statement if you are using a line of credit or credit card account.

The lenders want to see these statements and have proof on file of where the down payments funds are coming from.

Lenders will accept borrowed down payments as long as you declare and prove them.

There are other down payment sources

In all my years in the mortgage business I have seen down payments come from many sources some were unique, the sale of animals, dogs, horses and farm stock. I have seen the sale of planes and some rather interesting businesses all in the name of providing people with a down payment for their new home.

The best tip to remember is, make sure you have a complete paper trail of where your down payment is coming from. The more detail you can provide the better.

Mortgage Insurance: What it is and why you may need it

Mortgage insurance is a type of insurance that protects the lender in case you default on your mortgage payments.

You only need mortgage insurance when you are putting down less than 20% for your down payment. These types of loans are called **High Ratios Mortgages**. When you put down 20% or more for your down payment you are now in a **Conventional mortgage**. These are the current rules in Canada at this time.

The mortgage insurers all use the same premium schedule as listed below

With 5% down payment you pay 3.15% of the mortgage balance

With 10% down payment you pay 2.40% of the mortgage balance

With 15% down payment you pay 1.80% of the mortgage balance

Some lenders will insure conventional mortgages as well. It allow them to sell the mortgage off later to investors or other lenders. Banks and lenders will do this occasionally so they can get more money to lender in the future.

When they insure a mortgage it is guaranteed the investor cannot lose their money. In some cases the lenders will pay the premium themselves on conventional mortgages so that they can sell these in the future.

In some cases, clients may have damaged credit scores or the home may be in an area outside a city or town. This is a higher risk for the lender in case of default. Some lenders will ask that the mortgage be insured to protect them once again. If this is the case the client is then asked to pay the premium. The premiums are less as per below:

With 80% down payment you will pay 1.25% on the mortgage balance

With 75% down payment you will pay .75% on the mortgage balance

With 60% or more down payment you will pay .60% on the mortgage balance.

It should be noted the premium they charge can be paid in one of two ways:

1. You can pay it up front thus avoiding adding it to the mortgage and paying interest on it for years to come.
2. You can have it added to the mortgage balance and you will pay interest on the new mortgage balance.

Just to be clear, you have to pay these premiums when you are putting down less than 20% and in some cases even when putting down more as explained above.

What happens if I stop making my mortgage payments?

This is what the insurance is designed for. If you should stop making your regular mortgage payments the lender will contact you within days of a missed payment to help arrange a schedule to get back on track.

If you continue to miss payments the lender will begin a foreclosure proceeding against you. They must file a document in the courts and this takes between 4 to 6 months to go through the courts.

If you cannot make up the payments missed or renegotiate with the lender for terms that will work for you. The courts will issue a foreclosure decree on your home.

You will be forced to move out of your home and the bank will then sell the house. If after the sale is all done and all expenses are paid in full and there is any money left they will give this to you.

At this point the lender can make a claim on the insurance policy and they will be paid back every cent that is left owning on the mortgage.

The insurance company may or may not come after you for any losses they have incurred as there are many costs in doing a foreclosure, legal fees, sale commissions, maintenance fees while in the banks possession etc. These add up fast and normally absorb any equity left in the house.

The lender and insurance company force you to pay the premium for the insurance policy. The policy only protects the lender in case you default and you get to pay for this policy.

The only way to avoid this is to pay a larger down payment. Even then, you may be asked to pay a premium due to where you are buying or due to your damaged credit history.

If your credit is damaged then head over to my other site and learn how to repair and rebuild your credit. You can also get some great tips on how to maintain and ensure your credit rating stays good. There is a free book offer called Fix my credit NOW! You can get a copy at www.fixmycreditinfo.com

In Canada we have 3 companies that provide mortgage insurance they are:

1. **CMHC or Canada Mortgage and Housing Corporation** www.cmhc.ca
2. **Genworth Financial** www.genworth.com
3. **Canada Guaranty** www.canadaguaranty.ca

To find out more information on these mortgage insurers please visit their websites. They are loaded with great information and worksheets to help you budget for your new home purchase.

If you have questions you can also send me an e-mail at Daryl@maxmort.ca and I can try to help lead you in the right direction.

Mortgage Types and Terms: What you need to know

Depending on your situation you will find a variety of mortgage option available. **There are two main types of mortgages:**

1. Fixed term mortgages
2. Variable Rate mortgage:

With each of these types of mortgages there are also:

1. Closed mortgages
2. Open mortgages

Let's look at these in a little more detail:

Fixed Mortgages: OPEN and CLOSED

A fixed mortgage is normally set for a specific time periods from 6 month up to 10 years.

A fixed mortgage has a set interest rate for the term you agree on. At the end of the term you choose, the mortgage comes up for renewal. You then begin to renegotiate with the same lender or a different one, it is your choice.

Mortgages are normally amortized over 25 to 30 years in Canada

This means if you like 5 year fixed terms you would have 5 terms in a 25 year amortization period. You will be in negotiations at least 5 times during the life of the mortgage, unless you make pre-payments which we will cover later in this chapter.

An **OPEN fixed term** is normally for a 6 month to 1 year term. These are normally used when you intend to pay off the mortgage fast or sell it quickly once you own the house.

Interest rates are normally higher for these types of fixed mortgages as the lender knows you will only be in the mortgage a short time so they charge a premium interest rate to make it worth their while lending you the money.

I only recommend these when you have short term plans or are planning on flipping the house and selling quickly. With that in mind I normally always suggest the variable rate option instead as they are cheaper and charge a lower interest rate. If there are delays in your plans you can save money. You can also transfer the old mortgage to your new home in some cases.

The big advantage of an OPEN fixed term mortgage is that there is no penalty for paying off the mortgage sooner than the term you took. Let's say you pay the mortgage off half way through the term. Normally you will be charged a penalty of at least 3 months interest.

With and OPEN fixed term there are no extra penalty charges. The disadvantage is that due to this feature the interest rates are always higher than a CLOSED fixed term mortgage.

A **CLOSED fixed term** is set for a specific period say 5 years and during this term your interest rate will not change. Your payment stays the same through the whole 5 year term.

The CLOSED term means, if you break the mortgage before the 5 year term is up the lender will charge a 3 month interest penalty or can charge an Interest Rate Differential penalty or IRD penalty.

IRDs are the biggest problem we have in the mortgage industry. Each bank can set their own Posted rate and this is what the lenders will calculate the penalty from.

The only time an IRD penalty is charged is when the current interest rate is less than your contracted 5 year interest rate. The bank will then use this formula to calculate their loss since you are paying out the mortgage early. They will then charge you the IRD penalty.

For example:

Let's say you have a 5 year mortgage and you have 3 years left owing on the mortgage when you sell your current home. The interest rate is 5.70% on the 5 year term

Say you still owe $200,000 on the mortgage and the current interest rate is now 4% (so 1.7% lower than your current interest rate). This 4% is the POSTED rate of the lender you are working with.

The simple math is:

$200,000 remaining balance X interest rate difference 1.7% X 3 year remaining or $10,200.

So the IRD would be $10,200 compared to a simple 3 months interest penalty if your contract term rate is less than the current rate posted by your lender.

You can see how this can become expensive quickly if the new rates are lower than your current contract rate.

Variable Rate Mortgages: OPEN AND CLOSED

Variable rate mortgages are available in OPEN and CLOSED terms and usually in 3 or 5 year terms.

A variable rate mortgage means the interest rate will fluctuate (go up and down) in relationship to the Bank of Canada Prime Interest rate.

The Bank of Canada sets the prime rate every 6 to 8 weeks. Normally the rate will move in .25% increments but it can move in higher increments if the government sees fit to do this.

Each time the Bank of Canada moves the prime rate your bank will adjust your interest rate. They will send you a letter to state how much the rate has changed and what your new mortgage payment will be until the next rate change happens.

You want to use variable rate mortgages with lenders that allow you one free conversion back to a fixed term. This clause allows you to call the lender anytime during the term of the mortgage and request it be converted back to a fixed term.

You are required to convert back into a term equal to or longer than what is remaining on your current term.

The only risk with these mortgages is that when prime rates begin to increase the fixed rates have already begun increasing. Since fixed rates are based on the open Bond market they will reflect a rising interest period sooner than variable rates.

This means when you make the request to change to a fixed term. The fixed rates will have already been on the rise and will not be what the current fixed rates are. This has been what has happened in the past and will likely be the case in the future.

OPEN Variable Rate Mortgages:

These mortgages are based on the prime rate PLUS. Currently OPEN variable rates are at prime plus .80 to 1.00%.

The mortgage is OPEN which means no penalty is owed if the mortgage is paid out early.

CLOSED Variable Rate Mortgages:

These mortgages are based on the prime rate MINUS Currently CLOSED variable rate mortgages are at prime minus .50 to .60% off (currently).

The mortgage is CLOSED which means you will have a 3 month interest penalty similar to the fixed term mortgages. The good news is there is no IRD penalty as with the Fixed mortgages.

What other conditions and options are available with your new mortgage

Each lender has similar terms and conditions with their mortgages. The important items to watch for when looking at lenders and their mortgage options are as follows:

Pre-payment Options:

All lenders will allow you the privilege of making extra payments on your mortgage. They will have a variety of terms that you must meet to do this but in most cases as long as your payments are made on time as promised you can make extra payments.

Any extra payment you make will be credited to the principle mortgage balance. None of the money will be used to pay interest.

The lenders usually allow anywhere for 10 to 20% of the ORIGINAL mortgage balance to be paid each year.

You can pay anytime during the year and you can do it in a number of ways. You can increase your regular payment by 10 to 20%. Some lenders will allow you to double up each payment you make or you make bulk payments throughout the year.

You want to ensure any lender you use has a pre-payment feature similar to the one described above.

Transfer and Portable Option:

This option allows you to transfer your mortgage to another home once you have sold the current home that the mortgage is registered too.

If you transfer your mortgage to another home you can avoid any penalty on the old mortgage. It also can help you conserve your lower interest rate you may have. This option can save you thousands of dollars in penalties.

You are allowed to port the old mortgage to the new house. You can add more money to the old mortgage, but you must requalify to do this.

You can then blend your old interest rate with the current new interest rate which means you come up with a new rate somewhere in between the two rates.

Transferring your old mortgage can save you a lot of money in penalties and interest. It is well worth looking into once you own your own home and want to look at buying a new one.

Regular Payment Options:

Most lenders will allow you to make a variety of different choices for your regular payment. You can pay monthly, semi-monthly, bi-weekly or weekly. You can also use accelerated bi-weekly or weekly payments.

Accelerated payment options mean you will make extra payments each year. All of these extra payments will be credited to the principle balance of the mortgage.

With Bi-weekly accelerated payments mean you will make two extra payments per year. Weekly accelerated payments mean you will make 4 extra payments per year.

To really understand how much money you can save on your mortgage and other tips to help you save on your new mortgage please get a copy of my book called "How to Save Thousands on your mortgage"

You can visit my website at www.savethousandsonmortgage.com and download a copy. It's FREE and if you implement the tips you will save thousands on your next mortgage.

There are many other terms and conditions with a mortgage but these are the main ones you need to focus on. They can help save you a lot of money if implemented with your new mortgage.

Pre-approvals: Why you must get it in writing

A written pre-approval provides you with proof you have been pre-approved for a mortgage. It provides you with a rate hold for up to 120 days. This means your rate will not go up during this period.

A pre-approval also provides you with a list of conditions and paperwork requirements that you will require once you find your new home and have an accepted offer.

Before you even begin looking at properties you need to know how much you can afford. A written pre-approval will provide you with a piece of mind knowing that once you find your home you can afford to buy it.

A big issue I have with large banks and lending institutions is they will provide a verbal approval but not follow it up with a written pre-approval. This can be a real problem in a market where interest rates are rising.

I have witnessed this with clients in my mortgage business. Clients get a verbal approval from their personal bank and then a month or two later find a home. Only to find the lender will no longer give them the rate quoted at the time. Since they have nothing in writing they lose that rate and now must pay more for the mortgage.

Always get your pre-approval in writing

If your broker or bank will not put it in writing and take the time to have you complete a mortgage application and discuss your need you should run. Find someone who will put it in writing.

Your realtor will want to know if you have done this. You can show them your written pre-approval. This makes you feel better and certainly makes your realtor work harder as they know you are serious about buying a home.

Pre-approvals are easy to do and you are under no obligation

A pre-approval obligates the lender who issues it to you but you can still shop with other lenders in the future. They have provided you a written rate hold and will honor it if you find a new home and take possession before the expiry date on the pre-approval.

It is always fair to allow the lender who pre-approved you the chance to meet any better offer you may find. They believed in you from the beginning, as a broker I say this is the least we can do. Give them a chance to meet or beat the best rate you can get.

How do you get a pre-approval

You can get one through your bank or through a mortgage broker. You only need to complete a mortgage application. If you are self-employed you will be asked to provide your last 2 years tax returns to prove your current two year average income.

I have been doing mortgage pre-approvals for over 15 years and would be pleased to help you if you live, and/or want to buy in Canada. You can contact me at Daryl@maxmort.ca . We can arrange a time to talk or converse by email if you prefer. I would be pleased to meet with you if you are in the Calgary, Alberta Canada area.

If you want to get started immediately you can complete an application at my secured application page at www.maxmort.ca/applyonline

Click on my picture, Daryl Marsden and you will be sent to my private and secured application page.

Please note due to some browsers, please do NOT use your ENTER key when completing your application.

It can prematurely submit the application. Use your TAB key or Mouse to move from question to question. Once you hit submit it will be set to my computer and I can help you immediately.

Paperwork: What do I need to provide to a lender or bank?

This subject is a little more difficult to define as each lender may request a variety of different paperwork depending on the mortgage you are getting. I will review the basic paperwork and anything else a lender may ask for.

To be safe, I always suggest gathering as much paperwork as you can in case the lender asks for it. Below is a list of the basic paperwork you will require with most mortgage applications.

Income Confirmation: This section is very important and I devoted a whole chapter to it. So to summarize

1. You will need a job letter stating your position, salary and length of employment if you are an employee of a company.
2. You will need a copy of a recent pay stub that will confirm the information above.
3. It is always good to have your T4 slip from the previous 2 years available in case it is asked for.

This proves two things, one you have been working two years and two the income you stated on the job letter is true.

4. The **T4's also help to prove a 2 year average income if you work in a job with overtime or bonuses, so have these available if you are in a position that pays extra money**

5. **If self-employed you will need your last 2 years T1 General tax returns from Revenue Canada.**

6. **If self-employed you will need your Revenue Canada Personal Notice of Assessments for the last two years to confirm the government accepts your income on the application.**

7. If self-employed you may be required to provide a 2 year history of your business financials as well. It's a good idea to have these on hand.

Down Payment Confirmation:

This is another area I went over in detail in a previous chapter. To summarize:

1. If the money is in a bank account you need the last 90 days of bank statements proving where is has been sitting and that it is your money. So you need at least one statement that has your name and account number on it to link the account to you.

2. If in Investments. You need your last 2 quarterly or last 3 monthly statements to prove it is your money. Your name and account number must be on at least one statement.

3. If from sale of assets you need a full paper trail of the sale and then proof the money is deposited into your account.

4. If a gift from a family member, we need to have a gift letter signed by all parties and proof the cash is in your account.

5. If borrowed, we need a statement proving the interest rate and minimum payment you must make to service the debt.

If the down payment comes from another source feel free to e-mail me to discuss the paperwork lenders will require at Daryl@maxmort.ca

Personal Identification:

Most lenders rely on lawyers to gather this but we suggest always collecting at least one to two pieces of ID for all mortgage applicants.

1. Driver's license
2. Passport
3. Social Insurance Card
4. Government issued ID.

These are what we look for and they are acceptable to most lenders. If it has a picture it is a good ID.

A valid cheque from a bank account:

All lenders will require you to provide a cheque from an account they can withdraw your monthly payment from. You want to provide a copy of a VOID cheque.

A void cheque can do a few things for you.

1. Provides further ID proof
2. Connects you to your bank account
3. Saves the lawyer and lender having to get a copy at the last minute.

Proof of debts being paid:

Some lenders will require that you have some debts paid off in order to make the debt ratios work. If this is required on your approval or pre-approval you will need to provide proof of the original bill and amount owed. Then proof you have paid it off in full.

Usually this is a credit card or loan that must be paid down or completely off. We always suggest you send a copy of the last statement. Then proof you paid the bill on-line with an online statement.

Of course you will need to provide proof the online account is yours as well.

Separation or Divorce Paperwork:

Lenders must include alimony payments and child support payments in your debt calculations and debt servicing ratios.

If you are in a divorce or separation or have recently gone through one, you will be asked to prove you are owed or owe the alimony or child support payments.

It is very important to have a copy of these documents handy so you can support any claims you make on what you owe or what you are owed by your ex-spouse.

Do not expect the lender to just take your word for it. If you are in either of these situations or have recently gone through one on the last 5 years it is best to have copies of the agreements on hand.

It is important to make sure you have the signed versions on hand to confirm they are all legal and obligating to all parties.

You may be asked to provide 3 to 6 months bank statements that prove deposits from support or alimony payments.

Condominium Documents:

When you are buying a condo you will normally receive a binder with the by-laws, condo board meeting minutes, and the condo financials.

The lender wants to see these to confirm that the board has their finances in good shape. They want to see they have a reserve fund that will take care of future maintenance expenses.

The Reserve fund will predict future expenses and your condo fees will be used to help pay these future expenses.

On occasion there are special assessments made as an unexpected expense may come up. In this case, the board will assess a cost to each unit in the condo complex and each unit must come up with the extra cash to cover this cost.

These special assessments are normally uncovered by the lender by reviewing the condo documents and board meeting minutes.

If a special assessment is coming, you need to negotiate who will pay for this either you or the seller. Your realtor can be very helpful in these types of case.

There are companies that specialize in reviewing condominium documents. They go over all the by-laws and financials and then provide you with a written report as to what they have found. **The cost is around $400 to $500 per report. It is an expense that is well worth the investment as it can uncover some expenses you did not anticipate.**

Other property information:

If you own other properties you will need to declare these on your application. The lender will then ask for a copy of the property title to confirm you own it and how much may still owe on it.

They will ask for a recent mortgage statement to confirm the current mortgage and payments along with the interest rate.

If the house is free of debt they will require a copy of the title to confirm this.

If you own other property they will want to debt service any payment. Such as the mortgage, property taxes, condo fees and your monthly heating cost.

If you have the property rented out they will want to see a copy of a valid lease or tenant agreement that proves the rent you charge.

All of these expenses are taken into account on a new application.

If you are renting a property you own most lenders will allow you to use 50% of the income for your next purchase when qualifying. Each lender has specific policies and conditions for revenue properties. It is best to confirm with the lender.

If you own multiple properties, you really should not be reading this book now should you. Should this be the case, you will need to declare each property and provide the same information on each one.

Appraisals:

In some cases you will have to arrange to have an appraisal done on the property to prove its value. **This is normally arranged by the lender or mortgage broker.**

You will be required to pay for the appraisal and the normal cost (at the time of this writing) is about $350 to $450.

The appraisal must be ordered through an appraiser that the lender approves. This is why the mortgage broker or lender usually orders it.

Never order one yourself unless you have the lenders permission to do so. You may end up paying for two appraisals if you do this.

Home Inspections:

Lenders do not normally require these reports. They are done mainly for your benefit. I will go into more detail in a chapter later in the book.

We have had to supply a copy of a home inspections when a price reduction is made due to a problem or issue uncovered due to the inspection.

The lender wants to know the details of the issue and the inspection normal points this out.

These are the main documents lenders will request but as I mentioned each lender can make further requests for documents depending on the deal you make.

Having the paperwork all ready and set aside will make the whole process easier for you and the lender and your mortgage broker. Take the time to prepare your paperwork and review it with your lender or mortgage broker, you will be glad you did.

"A real estate purchase is very stressful and the more you have done to prepare for it the less stress you will experience. Trust me, I know this from experience, take the time to get all your paperwork in order you will be glad you did."

The 3 Types of Insurance with your mortgage

Mortgages require 3 types of insurance, each has its own purpose. Depending on your down payment amount you may need all three.

If you have a conventional mortgage you will not need the first type of insurance. If your down payment is less than 20% you will need to have mortgage insurance that protects the lender.

All mortgages will need the second type of insurance and it is highly recommended to have the 3rd type of insurance although it is not mandatory.

Let's look at the 3 types of insurance:

1. The first is Default Insurance: CMHC, Genworth or Canada Guaranty

This is the costly one, as you are required to pay this if you put less than 20% down payment on the house.

Depending on how large a down payment you put down, the premium will be reduced by the size of the down payment. The premium is calculated and is added to the mortgage amount as a onetime fee which they include as part of the total mortgage.

This insurance only protects the lender in case you default and stop making payments on your mortgage. If this happens this insurance allows the lender to make a claim and get all the remaining money back.

2. The second insurance is the fire and contents insurance:

You are required to protect the property in case of fire. The lender will be in the first loss position. This means if there is ever a fire the lender is paid first.

This type of insurance is usually taken care of by a general insurance company. The best advice is to call the same company as your car insurance as you can get a multi-product discount and it normally runs about $300 to $500 per year.

You must have a binder letter from your insurance company for the signing at the lawyers office just before your possession date.

3. The third type is Life insurance:

Life insurance coverage is completely optional. I always recommend that you have a separate life insurance policy that covers the full mortgage balance in case of you or your spouse's death. The house is completely paid off if either of you pass away. Any remaining funds are then paid to the surviving spouse or the estate. This can help with other expenses.

I always recommend getting a separate term life policy as it is the cheapest type of life insurance for most folks. You can get this type of policy from any life insurance planner.

I never recommend you take the lenders insurance, if you switch lenders at the renewal date, then the insurance collapses and you must re-qualify for a new policy. You are older and could have health issues that do not allow you to qualify.

A normal term life insurance policy will cover you for up to 20 years. Hopefully you will not need life insurance after that period.

If you buy a bigger house you can always add a term rider to the old policy to further protect you and your spouse.

Insurance is an important aspect of every mortgage. The second and third types can be shopped around competitively.

The first insurance has the same premium with all three companies. They all charge the same premium rate. Each company has a few special products for different types of mortgages. You bank or mortgage broker can place your mortgage with the one that best suits your needs.

Lenders normally make the choice for you but you are allowed to ask for a specific one if you want.

Purchase Plus Improvements: How can you renovate your new home?

When you are buying a home, sometimes you may want to do some renovations once you own the house. The Purchase plus Improvements program can provide you with this option.

The program allows you to add up to 10% of the purchase value in improvements. This means the house price will be increased so you need to pre-qualify for it at the new price.

Ex: you buy a home for $400,000 and want to do a deck or finish the basement for lets say $30,000. You would need to be pre-approved for $430,000 and your down payment is based on the new price.

These improvements must be permanent improvements to the home. You cannot buy furniture or appliances with this program. They must be permanent changes to the home.

The trick to the program

The program is great but has a couple of issues that can make it hard to take advantage off when needed.

You must have the estimates for all your renovations in writing and before you remove your financing conditions.

The contractor you hire to do the project must have the project 100% finished and inspected before any money is provided. This means you will need to cover any deposit the contractor requires.

You also must pay for the inspection with an appraiser. The normal cost is about $100 to $150.

You are allowed to pay for all the invoices yourself and then submit them once the project is 100% complete for inspections and payment. You can use credit cards or lines of credit or cash to cover these expenses.

Once the project is finished and inspection is done, the lender will then release the cash to your lawyer. The lawyer then cuts you or your contractor a cheque to cover the costs.

If you do not use all the funds in the estimates your mortgage is modified to reflect this.

A great program when you want new floors or the basement developed immediately.

You only need to be aware of the program details and how they work.

Making your offer to purchase

The fun begins! This is an exciting part in the process!

You found your new home, in your perfect neighborhood. You can picture yourself in the house, raising your family, relaxing in your yard enjoying the smells of a BBQ.

Now it's time to make an offer for your new home.

I cannot stress this next point enough; use a professional realtor to help you make your offer

I am not a realtor, but as a mortgage broker I have witnessed many deals go bad due to folks trying to do everything on their own. I have some sad stories that resulted in lawsuits and lost dreams and lost money.

There is no cost to have a realtor represent you on a purchase. In Canada the seller is responsible for paying the selling commissions. This means you have no cost to use a realtor when buying a new home only when selling a home.

Find a professional one and try working with that one person. Having multiple realtors is not needed as the professionals have access to the Multiple Listing Service and they can find every listing in your area that fits you requirements.

Realtors will protect your interests and can negotiate for you on your behalf. They can also refer you to other professionals that you will need, such as a lawyer, home Inspector or appraiser. Let them do what they do best.

Prepare yourself for the process

Once you make an offer things will move fast, very fast.

You will always add a term or condition that states you have 5 to 7 working days to get your financing approved and in place. This is a standard term with all offers. You should always have this written into your offer to purchase.

You may also want a home inspection or appraisal so you will want to have these conditions or terms written into the offer. The next chapter will cover those in detail.

These terms or conditions provide you time to get things done. The financing takes time so you always want this in your offer. If the house is older than 3 to 5 years you will want to get an inspection to ensure all is good with the house.

Now it's time to get the paperwork submitted.

As a mortgage broker I inform my clients of the paperwork needed on all pre-approvals and approvals. Once they are pre-approved I send a list of all the paperwork that will be required to complete their new mortgage.

In some cases the lenders may ask for something we did not predict but most deals require the same type of paperwork. My team tries to prepare our clients as best we can for all requests.

If you are self-employed, I always ask for the tax information up front before submitting for a pre-approval. I need to confirm the income the lenders and mortgage insurers will allow us to use from your personal tax returns.

We don't want you wasting your time so it is best to always confirm self-employed clients income upfront.

In some cases we do this with new employed people. The reason for this is to confirm if there is a probation period and how long it may be for.

Taking these steps up front ensures you will be aware of everything you will need to complete your new mortgage.

You have made your offer, now what?

Your realtor makes the offer to the seller or the seller's realtor. They normally have 24 to 48 hours to review and accept or decline or counter offer. If they make a counter offer, you are normally given the same time period to consider your next move.

Once your offer has been accepted in writing you are now on the clock. You have normally 5 to 7 days to get your paperwork reviewed by the lender.

The lender will submit the deal to a mortgage insurer if you are putting down less than 20% as they need that approval. This can take one to two days.

Your broker or lender will then submit the paperwork for review and confirmation. The lender will confirm your employment and review everything.

Any questions or concerns will be relayed to you through the broker or lender. They will let you know if you require any more paperwork.

Once all the paperwork is reviewed and confirmed you will be given a green light to remove your financing conditions. Your realtor will have you sign a waiver to this and present it to the seller's realtor or representative.

Some offers will require you put down a larger deposit once you remove your financing conditions; this will be the time to do so.

Your Deposit is now at risk!

Once you remove your conditions or terms of the deal and provide a signed waiver to this effect your deposit is now at risk if you should fail to complete the purchase of the home.

If you back out of the deal you can lose this deposit and possibly be sued if the seller has any losses on the future sale of their home.

Always ensure all your conditions are met before waiving your conditions

Once you have removed all your conditions you can start to pack and prepare for the move.

Call the utilities companies and update everyone on your soon to be new address.

Congratulations you are about to own your own home!

Home Inspections and Appraisals

Home Inspections

Home inspections are a very wise investment and should be considered on any purchase you are seriously considering.

They can point out any current or potential issues in your new home. Along with a written detailed report you will also get rough estimates of the cost of repairing any issues that are uncovered.

The estimated cost of a home inspection is between $400 to $600 plus travel costs if the home is located outside a major city.

It normally takes about 4 to 6 hours to complete a detailed inspection. The inspector normally requires 24 to 48 hours to complete the written report.

If issues are uncovered and are costly to repair, you may want to consider finding a different home or asking for some of the costs to be covered or completed before your possession. Just because you ask, it doesn't mean the seller has to accept your offer.

If the costs are less than $1000 most people will consider this as normal wear and tear and this will not be considered a new negotiation on the price.

Major issues may be discussed but the seller is not obligated to renegotiate the price or continue with the sale of the house. If you can't come to an agreement the deal may collapse.

The majority of inspections will uncover regular maintenance items or minor issues. It is always a good idea to review and consider them.

The report also acts as a guideline to things you will need to take care of in the first year of ownership.

Home Inspections are a good investment

This is money well spent on any home 2 years or older and should be considered and budgeted for. They can save you money and headaches in the long term. Older homes have future maintenance cost this is a fact of homeownership and must be understood. The home inspection can provide a good roadmap to the issues that you will face in the future.

Appraisals

Appraisals are normally required to establish the value of the home you are buying. They are normally ordered by the lender or your mortgage broker. Always consult them before ordering an appraisal

High Ratios Appraisals

When putting down less than 20% the lender will insure the mortgage. That premium will be your expense. It can be paid up front at the closing time and on the possession date or you can have it added to the mortgage and pay it over time with the principle and interest on the regular mortgage payment.

When a mortgage is insured the insurance company will perform their own appraisal normally at their own expense. The insurer may use an automated system that establishes a value on the property from past records and current market conditions.

Conventional Appraisals

When putting down more than 20% for your down payment most lenders will require a 3rd party appraisal done by one of their approved appraisal firms.

This is normally ordered by the lender or the mortgage broker you are using. You will be charged between $300 to $500 plus travel costs depending on where your new home is located.

What is involved in an appraisal?

Appraisals can be in the form of a complete property inspection and market comparison of recent sales with the same characteristics as your new home.

The appraiser looks at the size of the home and the number of bedrooms and bathrooms and if the basement is developed.

The look at the finishing's of the house and added features such as garages, landscaping and appliances such as hot tubs, saunas, pools etc.

The appraiser takes into consideration the current condition of the house and any major issues that could need repair soon.

Appraisals compare recent sales in the neighborhood.

Recent sales in the same area around your new home will help establish a baseline for the appraiser to begin estimating the value of the home. Lots of recent sales make it easy for them to establish the value.

Few recent sales make it difficult to establish the value and the appraiser may have to venture further out from your area to find properties with similar comparable features to use for their appraisals.

The appraiser uses all this information to establish a price

Using everything they have collected the appraiser will prepare a report that is normally 8 to 15 pages long. It will detail everything they measured and noted and will take the 3 to 5 best comparables found and use them to establish their professional opinion of the home value.

Take Note: Appraisals are not the actual final value of the home.

Appraisals are an estimated market value. You may be paying more or less than this value depending on the current market conditions in your area.

You could be faced with a situation where there are multiple people trying to buy the property so the market price may edge up and this means you pay more.

What if the appraisal comes in lower than you're agreed on price?

Things become interesting in this situation. You can try to negotiate the price once again with the seller. You can cancel the deal if this is done as a term or conditions of the purchase offer.

If you are in a competitive offer situation you may not be able to make an appraisal a term or condition. I never recommend doing this with a conventional deal. As you could be in for a costly error if the value comes in lower than you're agreed on price.

If the appraisal is lower, you could be faced with having to make up the difference from the purchase price to the appraised price in cash in order to close your deal

This means you have to come up with more money to close the deal. The lender will only lend on the appraised value of the home.

If you bought a house for $300,000 and the appraisal came in at $285,000 this means you must make up the $15,000 shortfall as the lender now will only lend based on the $285,000 price valuation.

You may be putting down a large down payment and could adjust the price but if the deal is high ratio and the value comes in lower you may have a hard time coming up with the difference.

Appraisals are critical to the lender so ensure you have one.

This is easy if you are putting down less that 20% as the lender will insure the mortgage and they will want some type of appraisal done to establish value.

If you are putting down 20% or more it is essential you get an appraisal done before removing your financing conditions. Not doing this can be a costly mistake.

Remember: you do not order your own appraisal

The lender will recommend appraisers that they will allow to be used. Normally they will make the arrangement.

What types of appraisals are there?

1. **Automated value systems:** CMHC and some lenders have software programs that take into consideration all the features of a home and the area they are in to establish a high and low value. If your home fits in this value range the house is

automatically approved and the insurer will issue an approval based on this value.

2. **The Drive by appraisal:** Not as bad as it sounds. The lender will send out an appraiser to drive by the property, maybe take some pictures and review the neighborhood. They will than prepare a regular market evaluation to establish the price.

3. **Full 3rd party Review:** The lender or insurer will have a 3rd party do a physical inspection of the property. The appraiser will measure and review all details, taking pictures of the house and surrounding areas. They will also take pictures of the comparables for the report.

Each insurer or lender may or may not require an appraisal but you have the option to get one done if you like.

Remember Appraisals are a good investment

Don't be afraid to request one and always get them when you are putting down 20% or more. The cost is worth every penny along with piece of mind knowing you are not paying too much for your new home.

Why you need a real estate lawyer

We all know just about all lawyers can take care of a real estate transaction. This is not the issue as many can follow the basic lender mortgage instructions and get the deal done and registered.

The issue is how smoothly will the transaction progress

Lawyers that specialize in real estate transactions normally have at least one paralegal or assistant to help prepare all the paperwork and inform the client of everything they will need to complete the mortgage documentation.

They prepare all the formal paperwork for the lawyer and arrange a time for you to come in and sign the paperwork. They inform you how much money to bring in to the closing meeting; this includes their fee and any remaining down payment.

You meet the lawyer, sign the paperwork and the paralegal makes sure it all gets registered with the local land titles office.

The assistant or paralegal is the key to your smooth transaction

The lawyer will take the credit but the assistant is the key to a smooth deal. They ensure all the details are taken care of and ready for the meeting between you and the lawyer. (to all my lawyer friends, I am saying this with tongue in cheek)

They ensure the paperwork is registered and ready for your possession date. Then they make sure all the money is paid to the seller's lawyer in a timely fashion on the day of possession.

The lawyer witnesses your signature and reviews your ID and reviews the new mortgage details with you. The assistant makes sure everything else gets done.

When you use an unexperienced lawyer who does all his own work you may find they miss a step or become overwhelmed by the time factor and close the deal late. You may get a great deal on the price but if the deal fails to close on time you face penalties and this can quickly eat any savings you may have received.

A good real estate lawyer is worth his weight

Don't be fooled, you may pay less for an inexperienced lawyer but using an established and experienced lawyer will save you time and money in the long run.

You can shop around for deals on the cost of a lawyer but make sure you are shopping for lawyers that are experienced and can do the job.

Look for referrals from your realtor or mortgage broker. They deal with lawyers every day and can normally provide you with at least one or two names to call and interview.

These referrals can and will save you money in the long term so don't try to be penny wise when dealing with a lawyer.

Closing costs and Legal fees and other future costs

All real estate transactions cost money and most people focus on the down payment. You as the purchaser are responsible for paying these costs and fees.

In fact the lender and mortgage insurer normally have a condition that you must prove you have these funds available for your new home purchase. Some lenders require proof of up to 1.5% of the purchase price to prove you have the funds available to close the deal.

You must prove these funds are in your account before removing your financing conditions.

Every real estate deal has additional costs

The regular closing costs for a real estate transaction are listed below:

1. **Legal fees:** The cost of a good real estate lawyer will be estimated between $1200 and $1500. This

is the average price of a good lawyer in Canada and should be the budget you prepare for.

2. **Home Inspection fees:** As described in previous chapters the cost for a home inspection will range between $400 to $600 plus travel costs.

3. **Appraisal fees:** As described they will range from $350 to $500 plus travel costs.

4. **Title Insurance:** We have not discussed this cost as in many cases it is included with the legal fees. Title insurance protects home owners in two areas. The first one, is to ensure the transaction closes on time. Using title insurance allows the lawyer to guarantee the title will transfer on the possession date with no issues. The second protection, allows the buyer to protect their equity in the property in case someone else attempts to commit a fraud against the property or you the owner. If this occurs the Title Insurance company will pay the legal fees to defend your rights in a court of law. Many lenders require this with every transaction.

5. **IAD: Interest Adjustment Date costs:** Sometimes you may take possession of a house on a day other than the 1st or 15th. The lender may push the start date or funding date forward to the 1st or 15th of the month. If paying weekly or biweekly you they may move this date to a Friday or Monday. If this happens you must pay the interest on the new mortgage for the few days'

difference. The lawyer will estimate the cost of this when informing you of the cash you need to bring into the closing meeting.

6. **Property Tax Adjustment costs:** Property taxes are normally due on June 30th of each year. This means that depending on your possession or funding date you may either owe the past owner cash for property taxes he has prepaid. Or the seller may owe you money for taxes he has yet to pay. Taxes are normally paid 6 months in advance and 6 months in arrears. The lawyer will normally figure this out for you and you will be informed of the costs before the closing meeting.

These are the normal closing costs in every transaction

Each transaction could have some expenses that are not accounted for but most transactions will have these costs and fees listed above.

The unexpected expenses are normally fall into the categories below:

1. **Late closing expenses:** Sometimes a transaction will not close on time for numerous reasons. Each day it takes to transfer the sellers cash to his account will cost you money. You will be the one that pays the bill.

2. **Lender legal fees**: In some cases the lender may charge their legal fees to your bill. This is not normally done but it can be done in some cases.

3. **Extra Lawyer legal fees**: Some lawyers will charge more for doing mortgages for some lenders due to more time involved in the transaction and more paperwork requirements. Lenders hate these extra charges from some lawyers but it does happen.

4. **Disbursement fees**: Lawyers have extra charges for transactions and these fees are added to the final fee they charge.

5. **Special Assessments**: Sometimes condos have special assessments for repairs on the building and these fees must be paid at closing as a requirement of the lender. This is not a normal expense but it has happened.

6. **Provincial Land Transfer Taxes**: Some provinces have special taxes assessed added to every transaction for people that have not lived in that province. Ontario and British Columbia have these assessments that normally range from 1 to 3% of the property value. **These taxes are not allowed to be added to the mortgage so they must be paid in advance at the possession date.**

The costs involved in a real estate transaction can add up so it is important to budget for them from the start. Having $2000 extra on hand is a very good budget number and as a mortgage broker I suggest this be your targeted budget for closing and legal fees.

Call ahead to get the estimated costs

It's a great idea to contact your lawyer well ahead of the possession date to get an estimate of the closing or legal fees so you are prepared for these costs.

Possession day

All your hard work has led to this day. Your possession day, congratulations!

When everything goes smoothly there is very little to do on this day other than a chat with your lawyer and the realtor.

You want to ensure the lawyer has transferred the new mortgage money and your down payment to the selling lawyer.

Once this is confirmed, the key to your new home is releasable by the other real estate company or the seller.

You can meet your realtor at the house and get the key. Once this has taken place you can move in.

When using experienced people this should be all that happens on the possession day. Inexperienced people can cause delays in any number of areas.

Some good advice

1. **Always keep in touch with your lender, mortgage broker and lawyer along with your realtor.** In the beginning you want to be talking to your mortgage broker and realtor to get the deal secured and approved. Than ensure your lawyer confirms they have everything they need about 2 weeks before possession. In some cases the lender has not yet sent the final mortgage instructions so you can help things along with a phone call or two.

2. **Use a Money Draft or Bank Draft for paying the lawyer your fees and the remaining down payment.** Do not use a cheque or certified cheque. It is best to talk to your lawyer and confirm how they want the cash brought into their office.

3. **Get your Fire Insurance in place once your financing conditions are removed.** You will need it as the lawyer will request it so best to get it done sooner and eliminate last minute surprises.

4. **Ask your realtor to double check everything is ready about 1 week before possession.** It never hurts to ask them to double check things. If there is an issue you have time to fix it before possession.

5. **Ensure your utilities and Cable Company are set up to begin on the possession day.** You will

need to rest near the end of the day and it's nice to have power and cable so you can sit in front of your TV for the night.

6. Confirm with your realtor that the keys are released on the morning of the possession day before heading to the house.

Its possession day and your house awaits, congratulations!

Summary

This book was written to help my current clients and future clients. While writing it I realized it would be helpful for anyone looking to buy their first home.

I hope it has helped you learn the processes that you will face when this adventure begins.

If you live in Canada I would be pleased to offer my services and that of my team to help you secure a great mortgage and interest rate. You can reach me in a number of ways:

Daryl Marsden AMP
Verico Maximum Mortgages Inc
E-mail: Daryl@maxmort.ca
www.maxmort.ca

Other books by Daryl:

How to save thousands on your mortgage 2ⁿᵈ Edition
Available at: www.Savethousandsonmortgage.com

Fix my credit NOW!

Available at: www.fixmycreditinfo.com

The Mortgage Benefit Program

Available at: www.mortgagebenefitprograms.ca

Resources

Credit Agencies:

Equifax:

    http://www.consumer.equifax.ca/ in Canada

    http://www.equifax.com/ in the United States

Transunion:

    http://www.transunion.ca/ in Canada

    http://www.transunion.com/ in the United States

Experian:

    http://www.experian.ca/ in Canada

    http://www.experian.com/ in the United States

Credit Repair Information:

    www.fixmycreditinfo.com

Fraud Help:

www.fbi.gov/scams-safety/fraud the FBI website

www.transunion.com/personal-credit/identity-theft-and-fraud/ one of the big 3 tips site

http://www.visasecuritysense.com/en_US/preventing-fraud.jsp Good tips from our friends at VISA

http://www.rcmp-grc.gc.ca/scams-fraudes/month-mois-eng.htm Canada's version of the FBI for helping with fraud info.

Mortgage approval and pre-approvals:

www.maxmort.ca (ask for Daryl Marsden)

Mortgage Calculators:

http://www.maxmort.ca/mortgage-calculators.htm

21061416R00061